city light
dave butcher

thanks

This is the first year that my wife Jan has worked full time in our photo business and it has made a big difference. City Light may not have happened without her support, encouragement and advice. As a result I give a huge thank you to Jan.

Thanks to Steven Brierley, and his colleagues at Harman Technology, for their continued support.

Thanks to Andy Oakey at 10th Planet, Sheffield for pulling everything together and keeping us on track using the same design that he created for Lake Light.

prints and further information

Prints of the photographs in City Light, and many other places, as well as further information are available from my business web site www.davebutcher.co.uk

city light
cities of the world...and buxton

dave butcher
Published in the UK by
Dave Butcher Photography
Briarwood,
Tunstead Milton,
Whaley Bridge,
High Peak,
Derbyshire,
SK23 7ER
www.davebutcher.co.uk

©2013 Dave Butcher Photography.
The images and text in this book are the copyright of Dave Butcher who asserts his moral rights to be identified as the author of the work. Copyright 2013.

British Library Cataloguing-in-Publication Data:
A catalogue record for this book is available from the British Library.

ISBN: 978-0-9555627-2-3
First edition 2013

Design and editorial production by 10th Planet.

Printed by Loop Print.

contents

introduction

My previous three books have been all landscapes so this book, of city photographs, is a departure for me. This page is my only chance to include a landscape in the book as one of San Francisco's best known landmarks is just outside the city.

I have always taken city and landscape photographs as the opportunities arose but mostly I was known for my landscapes. Since becoming a full time professional photographer in 2005 the balance has changed so that for the last few years we have sold more city photographs than anything else, so with the help of my wife Jan, we thought it was time to pull some of them together in a book.

The pictures in City Light are a small selection from my picture library, I have lots more images for every city listed and quite a few more cities and towns besides these. All images are from high resolution scans of my medium format film negatives taken between 1990 and 2012. The digital files were then edited to have a similar range of tones to my darkroom prints (yes, I still make traditional darkroom silver prints as well!).

The selection may appear a bit quirky and some cities have just one image while others have several. This choice balances a spacious layout with the range of different places. To see more visit **www.davebutcher.co.uk**.

The book is divided into four sections: UK, Europe, the Far East and America. There is an article at the back on city and night photography. The usual technical details on each photograph are also included at the back of the book.

Mostly the pictures are of the buildings and architecture, some very old, some very modern. One of the biggest groups of pictures are those taken at dusk or at night. This works really well with black and white and accounts for about half of the images here.

I have included quite a few arcades, especially older style ones like those dating back to Victorian years.

There are three Bridge of Sighs, Venice hosting the original one, plus Cambridge and Oxford. Bridges are a key feature of cities and there are some stunning designs so there are lots of these.

Finally, Buxton has been my local town since moving to the Derbyshire Peak District in 1988 and it has become a very special place to me. It was built up as a Georgian spa town in the late 1700s and expanded during Victorian times. Some of the notable buildings are included here. Buxton, the highest market town in England at 1000 feet above sea level, is the only place in the book that isn't a city!

Dave Butcher, January 2013

4. Opera House Front

5. Buxton Slopes, Shadows and Crescent

6. Buxton Crescent and Lamp

7. Pavilion Gardens Octagon from the Bandstand

england | buxton

8. Devonshire Dome

9. Turner Memorial and Town Centre at Night

england | buxton

11. Granary Wharf Canal and Crane

12. County Arcade Roof

13. City from Above

10. Thornton Arcade

england | leeds

14. Punt on the River Cam and Clare Bridge

england | cambridge

15. Backstreet Bicycle, Garret Hostel Lane

16. Bridge of Sighs, River Cam and St John's College

17. Albert Bridge at Night

england | london

18. Chelsea Bridge at Night

19. Covent Garden

20. Shad Thames and Butler's Wharf

england | london

21. Leadenhall Market at Night

22. Shard and City Hall Scoop at Night

23. Tower Bridge from Shad Thames

24. Shard and Tower Bridge

25. Tower Bridge and City Hall at Night

26. Burlington Arcade

27. Battersea Power Station and Pimlico Telephone Box

england | london

28. Gherkin from Mitre Street

29. St Paul's from
Millennium Bridge at Night

30. Lloyds Building at Night

england | london

31. Trinity Bridge

england | manchester

32. Urbis and Sign

england | manchester

33. Town Hall

34. Salford Quays Victoria Building and Mariners Quay

35. Castlefield Canal and Bridges

england | manchester

36. Salford Quays Lowry Bridge

37. Millennium Bridge and Sage at Night

38. Millennium
Bridge from Tyne
Bridge at Night

england | newcastle

39. Radcliffe Camera from St Mary's Church Tower

40. Bridge of Sighs, Bicycles and Hertford College

41. Christ Church College and Puddle Reflections

england | oxford

42. Edinburgh Castle at Night Panorama

43. Princes Street from Calton Hill

44. Edinburgh Castle at Night with Gravestones

scotland | edinburgh

45. Royal Exchange Square and Lights at Night

46. SECC, Finnieston Crane and River Clyde

47. Squiggly Bridge over the River Clyde at Night

scotland | glasgow

48. Altstadt at Night

49. Altstadt and River Inn Reflections at Night

50. Tivoli Gardens at Night

51. Nyhavn at Night

denmark | copenhagen

52. Eiffel Tower and Trocadero Statues at Night

france | paris

53. Eiffel Tower and Trocadero Statues

54. Notre Dame Infrared

55. Sacre Coeur Back Street

56. Passage des Princes Arcade

france | paris

57. Eiffel Tower and Trocadero Fountains

58. Petite France Reflections at Night

59. Petite France Reflections

france | strasbourg

60. Alte Oper and Fountain at Night

61. Skyline at Night

germany | frankfurt

62. Zuiderkerk and
Boat on Canal

netherlands | amsterdam

63. Keizersgracht Canal Bridges and Lights at Night

64. Magere Bridge at Night

65. Ha'penny
Bridge at Night

ireland | dublin

66. Statues and Rooftops Near the Roman Forum

67. St Peter's Square, Fountain and Fairground at Night

68. Colosseum and Moon at Night

69. Castel Sant'Angelo and Sant'Angelo Bridge at Night

italy | rome

70. Spanish Steps and Fountain at Night

71. St Peter's Basilica and River Tiber from Sant'Angelo Bridge at Night

72. Trevi Fountain at Night

73. Pantheon Roof Dome from Inside

italy | rome

74. St Peter's Basilica and River Tiber from Umberto Bridge at Dusk

75. St Peter's Basilica and River Tiber from Umberto Bridge

76. Gondolas

77. Gondolas on the Grand Canal

italy | venice

78. Grand Canal and Santa Maria della Salute

79. Bridge of Sighs and Gondola

italy | venice

80. Gondola Moorings

81. St Marks Basilica at Night

82. Rialto Bridge at Night

83. Ponte Postumio and River Adige at Night

84. Roman Arena at Night with Moon

85. Aker Brygge Building at Night

norway | oslo

86. Stortorget at Night

sweden | stockholm

87. Opera House and Moon at Night

australia | sydney

88. Darling Harbour at Night

australia | sydney

89. Strand Arcade

90. Sydney Tower and Christmas Star

91. Harbour Bridge and Opera Bar Brollies at Night

92. Opera House and Palm Trees at Night

93. Hong Kong from Kowloon

94. Hong Kong Skyline from The Peak at Night

china | hong kong

95. Auckland Harbour Reflections at Night

new zealand | auckland

96. Christchurch Cathedral at Night

new zealand | christchurch

97. Harbour Board Wharf Office

98. Carter Fountain and Oriental Bay

new zealand | wellington

99. Long Wharf in Winter

usa | boston

100. Charles River Bridge Reflection at Night

101. Quincy Market Trees in Winter at Night

61

102. Chicago River Promenade in Snow

usa | chicago

103. Chicago Skyline at Night from BP Pedestrian Bridge

104. Michigan Avenue Stairway at Night

105. Sears Tower in Cloud

106. Empire State Building from 5th Avenue

107. Flatiron Building

108. Brooklyn Bridge from Manhattan Bridge at Dusk

109. Brooklyn Bridge from Brooklyn at Night

110. Manhattan Storm Clouds from Staten Island Ferry

usa | new york

111. Central Park Lake Infrared

112. Chrysler Building, Flags and Lights at Night

113. Times Square at Night

114. Rockefeller Building and Tree Lights at Night

usa | new york

115. Mercer Street Fire Escapes

116. Fisherman's Wharf Pier 39 Merry Go Round

117. Modern San Francisco from Alamo Square

118. Transamerica Pyramid

119. National Gallery of Art

120. Washington Monument and Flags at Night

◄◄ 121. Capitol Building
Reflections at Night

◄ 122. Jefferson Memorial

city photography

I take my photographs using film cameras but most of this article applies to both film and digital camera users.

City photography to me is all about the buildings, bridges, architecture, patterns, shapes and of course the light. I use a similar approach to that used for my landscapes and try and take pictures with as few people as possible - not always easy in cities. I also keep images simple and as graphic as possible, less is more. This is even more important with black and white as there are no colours to help separate parts of the picture.

Don't settle for a scene if you arrive and it's not what you had hoped for whether it's the lighting, weather, crowds or construction work. Check out when it would be right and go back. If you can't go back walk around the location to find a way of making a different version of the shot or try a different time of day. In bad weather look for the small parts of a scene and take those, save the big views for better weather.

I could be blindfolded and dropped into any city and know that I will take some stunning shots. However, I also know that with a bit of preparation I could do so much more and, with the high cost of travel, it pays to do some planning before you leave. So for me with patience, persistence, planning, and an eye for a different perspective I can take the record photograph then look for something a little different to put a bit of myself into the shot.

Composition

As always, any black and white photograph relies on strong, compositional elements and dramatic lighting, not whether the colours are pleasing.

Look around for foreground interest rather than the blank patch of grass in front of you. Move around to find an angle that hides something you do not want in your photo. If it is a grey day look for something to put in the sky, like a lamp, to fill the blank space and add a bit of interest in an otherwise boring area of the image. Avoid trees and lamps partly overlapping a building or partly against the sky. If possible, put the entire tree or lamp either against a building or the sky. Any line in the urban landscape can be used as a lead in. Things that work well include the line of buildings, roads, paths, fences, rivers, bridges and so on, to lead the eye of the viewer from the edges into your image.

Try and keep walls vertical by going back far enough or using a wide angle lens. If this is not possible, go in closer and point your camera upwards to exaggerate the distortion of the verticals. This usually works best with wide angle lenses so that everything from foreground to the farthest point is in focus.

Reflections, either in glass, on water or on wet surfaces, day or night, can make effective photographs on their own or add to something you have already selected. Puddles, wet pavements or lights reflected on water at night are all things to look for. The Frankfurt building reflections image is an example of what you can look for, even with low light levels at night.

Decide if shadows, bright sunshine or a mix of the two is best for a shot that you have seen. Also, if you want sunshine then the time of year is important. Winter sun stays low in the sky and may not light your shot at any time of day! Use local maps and Google Earth to check what the time of day and year is doing to your possible photographs.

Water can make very effective images, this includes fountains, rivers, waterfalls or waves crashing on a beach with the city behind. Decide if you prefer to see water droplets or streaky water. For streaky water use 1/2 to 1/8 sec exposure. If you want to see mostly water droplets use 1/100 to 1/500 sec. For a mix of streaks and droplets use 1/30 or 1/60 sec. Use the zoom control on digital cameras to check whether the result is what you wanted. Film users if unsure have to bracket by taking a range of exposures.

Light trails at night can make or break an image. If you decide to include them then start the long exposure as lights come in to the frame and allow them to exit so the light streak is across the entire image. The image of Big Ben here is an example of this. On the other hand a light trail that ends abruptly part way across the image seldom looks good.

Research

Before you arrive in a new city spend some time researching the locations and the sort of photos that you can expect to take. Use Google Images, Google Earth, Google Street View, Flickr and other similar services to give you a quick overview. Picture guidebooks, like the DK Eyewitness series, are particularly good. Choose city guides that are pocket size, have a map and show the main attractions in pictures.

It's also useful to be aware of a few restrictions that you may come across in cities. Mostly this concerns the use of tripods but can extend beyond this.

Indoor photography using a tripod may also be frowned upon. If you are taking photographs as an amateur just explain this and you will often be fine.

For commercial photography it is useful to carry a personal liability insurance certificate and you should be prepared to apply for permits in advance under some circumstances.

Night Photography

Photography in the dark requires some different techniques to normal and a bit of patience. The best time to do night photography is at dusk before it gets completely dark. This gives a chance of detail in the sky and darker areas of your image. You need to wait for building and street lights to come on though or you will have a very dull picture!

Dusk doesn't last that long so know when it is and make the most if it. Once it's properly dark you can still take photos but you need to choose better lit subjects. Once dark, exposure times can be minutes not the more usual fractions of a second used during daylight hours.

To keep exposure times to a minimum it's best to use the largest aperture possible or just reduce it by a small amount. This means if your lens has a maximum aperture of f2 then use a setting between this and f4, for example.

If you are unfamiliar with the aperture scale here it is:

f2, f2.8, f4, f5.6, f8, f11, f16, f22

The difference between each pair of numbers, e.g. f4 and f5.6, is called 1 stop and is a doubling or halving of the exposure, depending on which way you make the change.

If you have worked out the exposure for a shot and then want to move further away remember that as you double the distance to your shot the exposure time will increase by 4x, not just double.

To avoid having to close the lens down to f22 try not to put anything close to the lens. For example all of my lenses have a maximum aperture of f4 so I try and use f5.6 or f8 for most of my night photography (the widest aperture of f4 is not as sharp as one or two stops closed down). It's important that you become familiar with your own lenses.

Long exposures have advantages as they can make otherwise busy pictures appear free of people, as long as they keep moving! For example, the front cover image was taken at about 8.30pm and it looks free of people. In fact there were quite a few people crossing Millennium Bridge but with a 2 minute exposure time and the fact that they did not stop they hardly registered on the photograph.

As the time when it gets dark changes through the year a photographer has to be both patient and adaptable. A bit of common sense is also needed so don't organise a night photography trip to the Orkneys or Scandinavia in June, for example, or you will be disappointed by the lack of darkness! In the summer taking night photographs means late nights. The Amsterdam night images in this book were taken in early July between 11pm and 1am. On the other hand in winter you can start taking night photographs from about 4pm in December.

There is also a difference in lighting levels between summer and winter. There tend to be more lights turned on in buildings in winter than in summer. Christmas is a good time for night photography as even poorly lit areas are often transformed into bright interesting subjects.

These days exposures can be left to cameras, especially those of the digital variety. Separate meters have limited

123. Sydney Monorail at the Galeries on Pitt Street

124. London Big Ben Light Trails

125. Frankfurt DZ Bank Reflected at Night

use at night but can be useful before it becomes truly dark. My Sekonic spot meters, for example, will measure exposures up to 15 seconds at f5.6 but for longer exposures they just show EU on the display. This is Sekonic suggesting I pack up and go home!

For fast lenses, the lower the f number (aperture) the more light that will reach the sensor or film. Using low f numbers, such as f2, will give shorter exposure times, a benefit for night photography.

To reduce your exposure times still further increase the ISO (sensitivity) to 800. If you go beyond this the noise that you will see in the image could be objectionable. Try it to see what you think. In summary....

Low ISO settings = slow shutter speeds
High ISO settings = fast shutter speeds but more image noise

Most digital lenses or cameras have some sort of Image Stabilisation. The name changes between different manufacturers, some call it Vibration Reduction for example, but they all do roughly the same job. They will let you take photographs handheld at slower shutter speeds than would otherwise be possible. Turn it on for handheld shots and turn it off when using a tripod.

Tripods are pretty much essential for night photography. At dusk you may be able to just about get by but once it is dark the exposure times can be of the order of minutes and no image stabilisation system can compensate for camera shake over these times.

Autofocus doesn't work very well in low light. The camera will continually try to focus which will rapidly drain your battery. Turn it off and use manual focus to avoid running out of battery.

At night, unless you find yourself under a street light it's difficult to check camera settings, focus, or find equipment in your camera case. A small led torch is invaluable to help you in such conditions. Even better is an led head torch with a red light. This is bright enough to let you change settings or find equipment but doesn't affect your night vision. A head torch also keeps your hands free. If you use a bright white light it will take a few minutes after turning it off to recover your night vision.

If you would like to include the moon in your night photographs it helps to use something like the Google Sky Map app for Android smartphones which predicts the position. This can be used on location too, you just load the application and hold your smartphone up to the sky and it will show the position of the moon over your location as you change the time.

Finally, combining more than one exposure in camera can also produce a little bit extra to your pictures. The Sydney monorail image here is actually 2 exposures on the same film negative. One exposure shows the train sitting in the station, the other gave the light streaks leading up to the train. If you want to do this work out what exposure you think will work, divide it by 2, use half of the exposure time for each exposure. With digital cameras you can of course also do this on a computer using 2 normally exposed images.

technical data full details of all the photographs in this book

PLATE	CITY	IMAGE	DATE TAKEN	FILM	CAMERA
1	Front Cover	St Paul's from Millennium Bridge at Night	4-Mar-2011	Ilford FP4	Mamiya 7
2	Frontispiece	Pantheon Roof Dome from Inside	3-Dec-2012	Ilford FP4	Mamiya 7
3	Introduction	San Francisco Golden Gate Bridge Waves Infrared	3-May-2008	Ilford SFX	Mamiya 7
4	Buxton	Opera House Front	1-Jun-2009	Ilford FP4	Mamiya 6
5	Buxton	Buxton Slopes, Shadows and Crescent	8-Apr-2003	Ilford FP4	Mamiya 7
6	Buxton	Buxton Crescent and Lamp	11-May-2005	Ilford FP4	Mamiya 7
7	Buxton	Pavilion Gardens Octagon from the Bandstand	1-Jun-2009	Ilford FP4	Mamiya 7
8	Buxton	Devonshire Dome	28-Oct-2006	Ilford FP4	Mamiya 7
9	Buxton	Turner Memorial and Town Centre at Night	8-Dec-2012	Ilford FP4	Mamiya 7
10	Leeds	Thornton Arcade	30-Apr-2012	Ilford FP4	Mamiya 7
11	Leeds	Granary Wharf Canal and Crane	30-Apr-2012	Ilford FP4	Mamiya 7
12	Leeds	County Arcade Roof	30-Apr-2012	Ilford FP4	Mamiya 7
13	Leeds	City from Above	30-Apr-2012	Ilford FP4	Mamiya 7
14	Cambridge	Punt on the River Cam and Clare Bridge	15-Aug-2003	Ilford SFX	Mamiya 6
15	Cambridge	Backstreet Bicycle, Garret Hostel Lane	27-Mar-2003	400 Delta	Mamiya 6
16	Cambridge	Bridge of Sighs, River Cam and St John's College	21-Jul-2006	Ilford FP4	Mamiya 6
17	London	Albert Bridge at Night	21-Apr-2012	Ilford FP4	Mamiya 7
18	London	Chelsea Bridge at Night	21-Apr-2012	Ilford FP4	Mamiya 7

PLATE	CITY	IMAGE	DATE TAKEN	FILM	CAMERA
19	London	Covent Garden	22-Apr-2012	Ilford FP4	Mamiya 7
20	London	Shad Thames and Butler's Wharf	14-Sep-2002	Ilford FP4	Mamiya 6
21	London	Leadenhall Market at Night	6-Mar-2011	Ilford FP4	Mamiya 7
22	London	Shard and City Hall Scoop at Night	20-Apr-2012	Ilford FP4	Mamiya 7
23	London	Tower Bridge from Shad Thames	27-Jul-2001	Ilford FP4	Mamiya 6
24	London	Shard and Tower Bridge	21-Apr-2012	Ilford FP4	Mamiya 7
25	London	Tower Bridge and City Hall at Night	20-Apr-2012	Ilford FP4	Mamiya 7
26	London	Burlington Arcade	6-Mar-2011	Ilford FP4	Mamiya 7
27	London	Battersea Power Station and Pimlico Telephone Box	21-Apr-2012	Ilford FP4	Mamiya 7
28	London	Gherkin from Mitre Street	22-Apr-2012	Ilford FP4	Mamiya 7
29	London	St Paul's from Millennium Bridge at Night	4-Mar-2011	Ilford FP4	Mamiya 7
30	London	Lloyds Building at Night	5-Mar-2011	Ilford FP4	Mamiya 7
31	Manchester	Trinity Bridge	2-Sep-2012	Ilford FP4	Mamiya 7
32	Manchester	Urbis and Sign	2-Sep-2012	Ilford FP4	Mamiya 7
33	Manchester	Town Hall	2-Sep-2012	Ilford FP4	Mamiya 7
34	Manchester	Salford Quays Victoria Building and Mariners Quay	2-Sep-2012	Ilford FP4	Mamiya 7
35	Manchester	Castlefield Canal and Bridges	2-Sep-2012	Ilford FP4	Mamiya 7
36	Manchester	Salford Quays Lowry Bridge	2-Sep-2012	Ilford FP4	Mamiya 7
37	Newcastle	Millennium Bridge and Sage at Night	11-Dec-2011	Ilford FP4	Mamiya 7
38	Newcastle	Millennium Bridge from Tyne Bridge at Night	11-Dec-2011	Ilford FP4	Mamiya 7
39	Oxford	Radcliffe Camera from St Mary's Church Tower	29-Nov-2012	Ilford FP4	Mamiya 7
40	Oxford	Bridge of Sighs, Bicycles and Hertford College	29-Nov-2012	Ilford FP4	Mamiya 7
41	Oxford	Christ Church College and Puddle Reflections	29-Nov-2012	Ilford FP4	Mamiya 7
42	Edinburgh	Edinburgh Castle at Night Panorama	1-Aug-2009	Ilford FP4	Mamiya 7
43	Edinburgh	Princes Street from Calton Hill	2-Aug-2009	Ilford FP4	Mamiya 7
44	Edinburgh	Edinburgh Castle at Night with Gravestones	1-Aug-2009	Ilford FP4	Mamiya 7
45	Glasgow	Royal Exchange Square and Lights at Night	25-Oct-2012	Ilford FP4	Mamiya 7
46	Glasgow	SECC, Finnieston Crane and River Clyde	27-Oct-2011	Ilford FP4	Mamiya 7
47	Glasgow	Squiggly Bridge over the River Clyde at Night	27-Oct-2011	Ilford FP4	Mamiya 7
48	Innsbruck	Altstadt at Night	7-Sep-2011	Ilford FP4	Mamiya 7
49	Innsbruck	Altstadt and River Inn Reflections at Night	7-Sep-2011	Ilford FP4	Mamiya 7
50	Copenhagen	Tivoli Gardens at Night	23-Sep-2009	Ilford FP4	Mamiya 7
51	Copenhagen	Nyhavn at Night	23-Sep-2009	Ilford FP4	Mamiya 7
52	Paris	Eiffel Tower and Trocadero Statues at Night	24-Jun-1995	Ilford HP5	Mamiya 6
53	Paris	Eiffel Tower and Tracadero Statues	23-Jun-1995	Ilford HP5	Mamiya 6
54	Paris	Notre Dame Infrared	23-Apr-1997	Ilford SFX	Mamiya 6
55	Paris	Sacre Coeur Back Street	25-Jun-1995	Ilford HP5	Mamiya 6
56	Paris	Passage des Princes Arcade	23-Jun-1995	Ilford FP4	Mamiya 6
57	Paris	Eiffel Tower and Tracadero Fountains	24-Jun-1995	Ilford HP5	Mamiya 6
58	Strasbourg	Petite France Reflections at Night	20-Sep-2011	Ilford FP4	Mamiya 7
59	Strasbourg	Petite France Reflections	20-Sep-2011	Ilford FP4	Mamiya 7
60	Frankfurt	Alte Oper and Fountain at Night	1-Sep-2011	Ilford FP4	Mamiya 7
61	Frankfurt	Skyline at Night	1-Sep-2011	Ilford FP4	Mamiya 7
62	Amsterdam	Zuiderkerk and Boat on Canal	5-Apr-2012	Ilford FP4	Mamiya 7
63	Amsterdam	Keisergracht Canal Bridges and Lights at Night	4-Jul-2012	Ilford FP4	Mamiya 7
64	Amsterdam	Magere Bridge at Night	3-Jul-2012	Ilford FP4	Mamiya 7
65	Dublin	Ha'penny Bridge at Night	27-Apr-2009	Ilford FP4	Mamiya 7
66	Rome	Statues and Rooftops near the Roman Forum	3-Dec-2012	Ilford FP4	Mamiya 7
67	Rome	St Peter's Square, Fountain and Fairground at Night	2-Dec-2012	Ilford FP4	Mamiya 7
68	Rome	Colosseum and Moon at Night	1-Dec-2012	Ilford FP4	Mamiya 7
69	Rome	Castel Sant'Angelo and Sant'Angelo Bridge at Night	2-Dec-2012	Ilford FP4	Mamiya 7
70	Rome	Spanish Steps and Fountain at Night	2-Dec-2012	Ilford FP4	Mamiya 7
71	Rome	St Peter's Basilica and River Tiber from Sant'Angelo Bridge at Night	2-Dec-2012	Ilford FP4	Mamiya 7
72	Rome	Trevi Fountain at Night	2-Dec-2012	Ilford FP4	Mamiya 7
73	Rome	Pantheon Roof Dome from Inside	3-Dec-2012	Ilford FP4	Mamiya 7
74	Rome	St Peter's Basilica and River Tiber from Umberto Bridge at Dusk	2-Dec-2012	Ilford FP4	Mamiya 7

PLATE	CITY	IMAGE	DATE TAKEN	FILM	CAMERA
75	Rome	St Peter's Basilica and River Tiber from Umberto Bridge	2-Dec-2012	Ilford FP4	Mamiya 7
76	Venice	Gondolas	15-Mar-1990	Ilford XP2	Mamiya 645
77	Venice	Gondolas on the Grand Canal	19-Mar-1995	Ilford FP4	Mamiya 6
78	Venice	Grand Canal and Santa Maria della Salute	15-Mar-1990	Ilford FP4	Mamiya 645
79	Venice	Bridge of Sighs and Gondola	19-Mar-1995	Ilford FP4	Mamiya 6
80	Venice	Gondola Moorings	18-Mar-1995	Ilford FP4	Mamiya 6
81	Venice	St Marks Basilica at Night	17-Mar-1995	Ilford HP5	Mamiya 6
82	Venice	Rialto Bridge at Night	18-Mar-1995	Ilford FP4	Mamiya 6
83	Verona	Ponte Postumio and River Adige at Night	13-Sep-2011	Ilford FP4	Mamiya 7
84	Verona	Roman Arena at Night with Moon	13-Sep-2011	Ilford FP4	Mamiya 7
85	Oslo	Aker Brygge Building at Night	24-Sep-2009	Ilford FP4	Mamiya 7
86	Stockholm	Stortorget at Night	4-Oct-2009	Ilford FP4	Mamiya 7
87	Sydney	Opera House and Moon at Night	17-Nov-2010	Ilford FP4	Mamiya 7
88	Sydney	Darling Harbour at Night	23-Oct-2010	Ilford FP4	Mamiya 7
89	Sydney	Strand Arcade	18-Nov-2010	Ilford FP4	Mamiya 7
90	Sydney	Sydney Tower and Christmas Star	17-Nov-2010	Ilford FP4	Mamiya 7
91	Sydney	Harbour Bridge and Opera Bar Brollies at Night	24-Oct-2010	Ilford FP4	Mamiya 7
92	Sydney	Opera House and Palm Trees at Night	24-Oct-2010	Ilford FP4	Mamiya 7
93	Hong Kong	Hong Kong from Kowloon	21-Oct-2010	Ilford FP4	Mamiya 7
94	Hong Kong	Hong Kong Skyline from The Peak at Night	21-Oct-2010	Ilford FP4	Mamiya 7
95	Auckland	Auckland Harbour Reflections at Night	26-Oct-2010	Ilford FP4	Mamiya 7
96	Christchurch	Christchurch Cathedral at Night	14-Nov-2010	Ilford FP4	Mamiya 7
97	Wellington	Harbour Board Wharf Office	1-Nov-2010	Ilford FP4	Mamiya 7
98	Wellington	Carter Fountain and Oriental Bay	31-Oct-2010	Ilford FP4	Mamiya 7
99	Boston	Long Wharf in Winter	4-Feb-2009	Ilford FP4	Mamiya 7
100	Boston	Charles River Bridge Reflection at Night	2-Feb-2009	Ilford FP4	Mamiya 7
101	Boston	Quincy Market Trees in Winter at Night	2-Feb-2009	Ilford FP4	Mamiya 7
102	Chicago	Chicago River Promenade in Snow	10-Jan-2009	Ilford FP4	Mamiya 7
103	Chicago	Chicago Skyline at Night from BP Pedestrian Bridge	10-Jan-2009	Ilford FP4	Mamiya 7
104	Chicago	Michigan Avenue Stairway at Night	10-Jan-2009	Ilford FP4	Mamiya 7
105	Chicago	Sears Tower in Cloud	21-May-2008	Ilford FP4	Mamiya 7
106	New York	Empire State Building from 5th Avenue	21-May-2008	Ilford FP4	Mamiya 7
107	New York	Flatiron Building	21-May-2008	Ilford FP4	Mamiya 7
108	New York	Brooklyn Bridge from Manhattan Bridge at Dusk	21-May-2008	Ilford FP4	Mamiya 7
109	New York	Brooklyn Bridge from Brooklyn at Night	21-May-2008	Ilford FP4	Mamiya 7
110	New York	Manhattan Storm Clouds from Staten Island Ferry	22-May-2008	Ilford FP4	Mamiya 7
111	New York	Central Park Lake Infrared	17-May-2008	Ilford SFX	Mamiya 7
112	New York	Chrysler Building, Flags and Lights at Night	15-Jan-2010	Ilford FP4	Mamiya 7
113	New York	Times Square at Night	20-May-2008	Ilford FP4	Mamiya 7
114	New York	Rockefeller Building and Tree Lights at Night	1-Feb-2010	Ilford FP4	Mamiya 7
115	New York	Mercer Street Fire Escapes	15-Jan-2010	Ilford FP4	Mamiya 7
116	San Francisco	Fisherman's Wharf Pier 39 Merry Go Round	15-May-2008	Ilford SFX	Mamiya 7
117	San Francisco	Modern San Francisco from Alamo Square	2-May-2008	Ilford FP4	Mamiya 7
118	San Francisco	Transamerica Pyramid	2-May-2008	Ilford FP4	Mamiya 7
119	Washington DC	National Gallery of Art	18-May-1990	Ilford HP5	Mamiya 645
120	Washington DC	Washington Monument and Flags at Night	28-Dec-2011	Ilford FP4	Mamiya 7
121	Washington DC	Capitol Building Reflections at Night	28-Dec-2011	Ilford FP4	Mamiya 7
122	Washington DC	Jefferson Memorial	29-Dec-2011	Ilford FP4	Mamiya 7
123	City Photography	Sydney Monorail at the Galeries on Pitt Street	17-Nov-2010	Ilford FP4	Mamiya 7
124	City Photography	London Big Ben Light Trails	21-Apr-2012	Ilford FP4	Mamiya 7
125	City Photography	Frankfurt DZ Bank Reflected at Night	1-Sep-2011	Ilford FP4	Mamiya 7
126	Rear Cover	Hong Kong Skyline from The Peak at Night	21-Oct-2010	Ilford FP4	Mamiya 7